THE BIG BITE BOOK OF BURGERS

MEG JANSZ

SMITHMARK

This edition published in 1994 by
SMITHMARK Publishers Inc.,
16 East 32nd Street,
New York, NY 10016.

1 2 3 4 5 6 7 8 9

SMITHMARK books are available for bulk purchase
for sales promotion and premium use. For details
write or call the manager of special sales,
SMITHMARK Publishers Inc.,
16 East 32nd Street, New York,
NY 10016; (212) 532-6600.

ISBN: 0-8317-0715-1

Printed in Singapore

CREDITS
Author and home economist: Meg Jansz
Home economist's assistants: Nicole
    Szabason and Cara Hobday
Managing editor: Lisa Dyer
Photographer: Ken Field
Designer: Paul Johnson
Stylist: Marian Price
Copy editor: Alison Leach
Filmset: SX Composing Ltd, England
Color Separation: P&W Graphics Pte, Ltd,
    Singapore

CONTENTS

INTRODUCTION   6

MARINADES & CONDIMENTS   10

CLASSIC BURGERS   18

FROM THE TURF   28

FROM THE SURF   48

MEATLESS WONDERS   58

SIDE ORDERS   70

INDEX   80

INTRODUCTION

The Big Bite Book of Burgers celebrates this favorite food which is a meal in itself – big, juicy burgers – but brings an international flavor to the humble burger by using a wide range of ingredients and seasonings.

Although America is credited with creating the burger, ground beef on bread was a specialty of Hamburg, Germany, which is how the hamburger got its name. The burger, as we know it, was reputedly first served by German settlers in America during the 1904 St Louis International Exposition. Although ground beef is still the favored ingredient, fish and vegetarian burgers increasingly have their place in today's more healthy lifestyle.

THE BASIC INGREDIENTS

To many people a burger is synonymous with ground beef; however, a wide range of basic ingredients can be made into a patty and eaten as a burger. Ground chicken, pork, lamb, turkey, veal and even venison make wonderfully tasty burgers, and fish and seafood can also be combined for unusual concoctions. For the vegetarian, rice, potato, beans and grains provide diverse starting points.

Ground beef is easily found in supermarkets, but you may have to visit a butcher for more unusual meats. A good butcher will also grind the meat to order for you. If you have a grinder, you can grind meat at home, but do not try to 'grind' meat in a processor. This will produce a solid texture, rather than the ideal grainy-meat burger.

Fish and vegetarian burgers, on the other hand, respond well to food processors. The texture of these ingredients is usually more

delicate, and so needs a certain amount of processing to make everything bind together.

Good seasoning is vital for all burgers. To your basic ingredient, add generous amounts of complementary spices, herbs and seasonings. Ideally, cook a small amount of the burger mixture in a skillet, taste it, and adjust the seasoning as necessary before you shape and cook the whole batch of burgers.

After you have combined the basic ingredients, shape your burgers into round patties, handling them as little as possible. This will insure a lighter textured burger, rather than a tough, dense burger. Ideally burgers should be about ¾-inch thick.

ADVANCED PREPARATION

Meat and fish burgers benefit from being prepared a short while before cooking. If you need to prepare them far in advance, try using one of the marinades on page 10. To do this, place the burgers in a shallow dish, brush them with the marinade, pouring the remaining marinade over, cover with plastic wrap, and refrigerate for 2 hours or overnight.

Marinating seafood burgers that contain breadcrumbs or cheese is not recommended, as the burgers will become soggy. Also avoid marinating the vegetarian burgers in the *Meatless Wonders* chapter, as they could disintegrate. Do, however, make the vegetarian burgers several hours ahead of time and chill them. Refrigeration will help to make them easier to handle during cooking.

RIGHT: Broiling or barbecuing gives burgers a charred outside while the inside remains moist.

STORING BURGERS

Burgers should not be refrigerated for more than 24 hours before cooking. If you absolutely must freeze burgers, arrange the uncooked, prepared patties in a single layer on a tray, and freeze them, uncovered, for 1–2 hours, or until they are hard. Then store the patties in freezer-proof boxes with wax paper layered between them. Meat and poultry burgers will freeze best, but burgers made from such ingredients as rice and lentils are fragile, and will always be better freshly made. Do not freeze burgers for more than three months.

COOKING BURGERS

Burgers can be cooked in several ways: barbecuing or broiling, pan-frying and deep-frying. The golden rule for cooking burgers is never to press them with a spatula, as their flavorsome juices would be lost.

All the meat burgers in this book will barbecue happily, as will those fish and seafood burgers which the recipes say are suitable for pan-frying. However, the fish and seafood burgers need to be handled with extra care. For best results, those fish and seafood burgers for which deep-frying is recommended should only be cooked in this way. Vegetarian burgers will fall apart on a barbecue, and must be cooked as directed in the individual recipes.

When barbecuing or broiling, place the burgers on oiled racks, and cook them quickly over hot coals or under a hot broiler. For barbecuing, insure that the coals have reached the glowing ash stage. Quick cooking will insure a charred outside and a moist center. Of course, non-beef meat or poultry burgers will require longer cooking, so they are well-cooked right through to the center.

Pan-frying is a quick and easy method that is available throughout the whole year. Use a heavy-bottomed skillet that has been well-oiled, and cook the burgers over a fairly high heat to achieve similar results to barbecuing or broiling. To deep-fry burgers, pour 3-4 inches of a good tasteless oil, such as corn, sunflower or vegetable oil, into a deep pan. To test if the oil is hot enough, drop a breadcrumb into the oil. If it floats and bubbles appear, the oil is the correct temperature.

As a general guideline for ground beef burgers, barbecue, broil or pan-fry the burgers for 4 minutes on each side for a medium-rare burger. Allow 5 minutes per side for a medium burger, and 6 minutes for a well-done burger. These guidelines will need to be adjusted according to the size of your burgers and the cooking heat.

BREAD, BUNS & ACCOMPANIMENTS

The obvious partner to a burger is a sesame seed bun; however many unusual breads and buns are recommended in the following recipes. For example, focaccia and ciabatta bread complement Italian-style burgers while pita breads can be used for Mediterranean-style burgers. Chinese pancakes, crêpes and soft flour tortillas make interesting choices, as do muffins and bagels. But none of the suggestions on the following pages is set in stone. Experiment with the breads available to you to create your own combinations.

Because many people prefer to eat accompaniments alongside their burgers, a selection of recipes for salads, chips and fries have been included in the last chapter, *Side Orders*.

RIGHT: Choose from a range of international breads bought from your local supermarket, specialty store or those you have made yourself.

MARINADES & CONDIMENTS

Burgers can be given exciting flavors by marinating them prior to cooking, and condiments, such as salsas and relishes, add a different texture to a burger in a bun. The recipes in this chapter are referred to in the specific burger recipes throughout the book, and all the marinades are of sufficient quantity for four burgers. Because tomato sauce and mustard are staples in most households, more exotic recipes are included here, such as Pumpkin Relish and Tropical Mango Salsa, along with suggested flavorings for mayonnaise.

LEMON MARINADE

¾ cup sunflower oil
Grated zest and juice of 1 small lemon
½ teaspoon cracked black pepper
2 tablespoons chopped fresh dill

To make the marinade, place all the ingredients in a bowl, and mix well to combine. Use as required to marinate burgers. Repeat this process for all the marinade variations opposite.

TANGY MARINADE

¾ cup grapeseed oil
Grated zest and juice of 1 lime
3 tablespoons finely chopped cilantro

MEDITERRANEAN MARINADE

¾ cup olive oil
1 tablespoon sun-dried tomato paste
2 cloves garlic, crushed
1 teaspoon chopped fresh oregano
1 tablespoon chopped fresh thyme

CHINESE MARINADE

1 tablespoon sesame oil
3 tablespoons sunflower oil
4 tablespoons soy sauce
2 tablespoons clear honey
2 teaspoons Chinese five-spice powder
2 cloves garlic, crushed
1 stalk fresh lemon grass, finely chopped

TANDOORI MARINADE

½ cup thin natural yogurt
2 teaspoons garam masala
1 teaspoon ground cumin
½ teaspoon chili powder
½ teaspoon turmeric
3 tablespoons chopped fresh mint

CLOCKWISE AND CENTER: Tandoori Marinade, Tangy Marinade, Mediterranean Marinade, Chinese Marinade, Lemon Marinade

MAYONNAISE

2 egg yolks
1 teaspoon Dijon mustard
Salt and ground black pepper
Pinch of superfine sugar
1¼ cups olive oil
2 tablespoons white wine vinegar

Place the egg yolks in a bowl, and whisk until thick. Stir in the mustard, seasoning and sugar; beat to combine.

Add the oil, drop by drop, whisking well between each addition. Each drop of oil should be thoroughly absorbed before more is added. As the mayonnaise thickens and becomes shiny, the oil may be added in a thin stream. Finally, blend in the vinegar.

If you prefer, make the mayonnaise in a food processor by blending together the egg and seasonings, then pouring in the oil in a steady stream until the mayonnaise is thick and shiny. Lastly, blend in the vinegar.

Store the mayonnaise in a covered jar in the refrigerator, and use as required.

SWEET PEPPER MAYONNAISE

6 tablespoons mayonnaise
3 tablespoons diced mixed bell peppers
1-2 tablespoons chopped fresh cilantro

Mix all the ingredients together. Cover and chill until needed. Use as required. Follow this method for all the variations below.

CHILI MAYONNAISE

½ cup mayonnaise
½ red chili, seeded and chopped
½ green chili, seeded and chopped
1 teaspoon chili sauce

GARLIC MAYONNAISE

½ cup mayonnaise
2 cloves garlic, crushed

HERB MAYONNAISE

½ cup mayonnaise
2 tablespoons chopped mixed herbs, or use a single herb of your choice

MUSTARD MAYONNAISE

½ cup mayonnaise
2 tablespoons Dijon or coarse-grain mustard

SESAME MAYONNAISE

½ cup mayonnaise
1 teaspoon sesame oil
½ teaspoon toasted sesame seeds

TOMATO MAYONNAISE

½ cup mayonnaise
2 teaspoons sun-dried tomato paste

CLOCKWISE: Chili Mayonnaise, Herb Mayonnaise, Sesame Mayonnaise, Sweet Pepper Mayonnaise, Mustard Mayonnaise

TANGY TOMATO SALSA

2 ripe beef tomatoes
½ small green bell pepper, seeded
I small shallot, very finely chopped
2 tablespoons chopped fresh cilantro
Freshly squeezed juice of I lime
Salt and ground black pepper
Pinch of superfine sugar

Cut the tomatoes into small cubes, and place them in a bowl. Dice the pepper finely, and add this to the bowl of tomatoes, together with the other ingredients. Toss gently to combine. Cover and chill for I hour before serving to allow the flavors to develop.
SERVES 4-6

TROPICAL MANGO SALSA

I small mango, peeled and finely chopped
¾ cup seeded and roughly chopped black grapes
2 slices fresh pineapple, finely diced
Pulp of I passion fruit
I fresh green chili, seeded and sliced
Grated zest and juice of I lime

Place all the ingredients in a bowl, and toss gently to combine. Chill the mango salsa for 2-3 hours before serving to allow the flavors to develop. SERVES 4-6

CRANBERRY RELISH

½ cup cranberry sauce
I tablespoon golden raisins
I tablespoon chopped fresh thyme
I orange, segmented and coarsely chopped

Place all the ingredients in a bowl, and toss gently to combine. Chill and use as required. SERVES 4-6

CUCUMBER RELISH

½ cucumber, peeled and thinly sliced
I large red chili, seeded and sliced
I shallot, finely chopped
2 tablespoons rice wine vinegar
I teaspoon superfine sugar

Place all the ingredients in a bowl, and toss gently to combine. Chill and use as required. SERVES 4-6

CLOCKWISE: Tropical Mango Salsa, Cranberry Relish, Cucumber Relish, Tangy Tomato Salsa

TOMATO RELISH

2 pounds ripe tomatoes
I medium onion
I teaspoon allspice berries, cracked
8 whole celery leaves
Scant ½ cup red wine vinegar
I teaspoon cayenne pepper
I tablespoon mustard seeds
⅔ cup brown sugar
Salt to taste

Wash and quarter the tomatoes, and place them in a heavy-bottomed saucepan. Dice the onion and separate it into layers. Add these to the pan, together with the allspice berries and celery leaves. Cover the pan, and cook the tomato mixture over a low heat for 45 minutes.

Uncover the pan, and add the vinegar, cayenne, mustard seeds, sugar and salt to the cooked tomatoes. Stir gently to mix in these ingredients, and cook the relish, uncovered, for a further 35 minutes, until it is pulpy and the juices are reduced and thickened.

Pour the hot relish into warmed, sterilized jars, let cool slightly, then seal and label. This relish will keep well for a month. After opening, store the relish in the refrigerator.   MAKES ABOUT 2 POUNDS

PUMPKIN RELISH

3 pounds pumpkin, peeled, seeded and cubed
Salt
2-inch piece fresh ginger root, peeled and grated
8 ounces shallots, peeled and sliced
1⅓ cups brown sugar
I small green bell pepper, seeded and cubed
I small red bell pepper, seeded and cubed
8 ounces cooking apples, peeled, cored and chopped
⅔ cup raisins
1¼ cups cider vinegar
½ teaspoon cracked black pepper

Place the pumpkin in a bowl, sprinkle over some salt to coat the pumpkin cubes, and leave overnight.

The next day, drain off the liquid, and rinse the pumpkin in cold water. Place the pumpkin in a large preserving pan with the remaining ingredients. Bring the mixture to a boil, then reduce the heat and simmer for about I hour, until the mixture is soft and pulpy.

Cool the mixture slightly. Then pack the relish into warmed, sterilized jars, and seal and label. The relish will keep for several months. After opening, store in the refrigerator.   MAKES ABOUT 3 POUNDS

TOP: Pumpkin Relish
BOTTOM: Tomato Relish

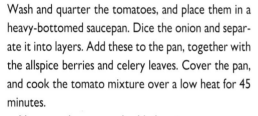

CLASSIC BURGERS

The recipes in this chapter all owe their inspiration to American-style burgers. Along with the standard Cheeseburger, there are more varied burgers, such as the Hickory Barbecue Burger and the Chili Burger. All of the recipes contain ground beef as their main ingredient. The best beef burgers are made with beef that has a little fat included, which creates juicy burgers.

CLASSIC HAMBURGERS

1½ pounds medium- or coarse-ground beef
Salt and ground black pepper
4 sesame seed buns, split lengthwise
A little butter, softened
Sliced onion
Shredded iceberg lettuce
Dijon mustard, dill pickles and tomato ketchup, to serve

Place the beef and seasoning in a bowl, and combine. Divide the mixture into four equal portions, and shape into patties to fit the buns.

Prepare a barbecue, broiler or pan for cooking the burgers. Brush the rack or pan with a little oil, and cook the burgers, turning once with a large spatula. Cook for 4 minutes on each side for a medium-rare burger, or longer. Toward the end of cooking, butter the cut sides of the buns, and broil to toast lightly.

To serve, divide the onion slices and lettuce between the four bottom bun halves. Place a burger on each, and finish with the bun tops. Pass condiments separately.   SERVES 4

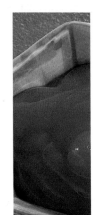

CHEESEBURGERS

1½ medium- or coarse-ground beef
Salt and ground black pepper
4 teaspoons Worcestershire sauce
4 slices American or Cheddar cheese
A little butter, softened
4 sesame seed buns, split lengthwise
Soft lettuce leaves
Sliced dill pickles
Sliced tomatoes
Sliced onion
Tomato ketchup

Place the beef, seasoning and Worcestershire sauce in a bowl, and mix well to combine. Divide the mixture into four equal portions, and shape into patties to fit the buns.

Prepare a barbecue, broiler or pan for cooking the burgers. Brush the rack or pan with a little oil, and cook the burgers, turning once with a large spatula. Cook for 4 minutes on each side for a medium-rare burger, or longer if a more thoroughly cooked burger is required. Just before the burgers are ready, top each one with a slice of cheese and let the cheese melt.

Toward the end of cooking, butter the cut sides of the buns, and broil to toast lightly.

To serve, divide the lettuce between the four bottom halves of the buns. Place a burger on each, top with dill pickles, tomatoes, onion and ketchup, and finish with the bun tops. Serve at once.   SERVES 4

RIGHT: Classic Hamburger

BACON CHEESEBURGERS

1½ pounds medium- or coarse-ground beef
Salt and ground black pepper
4 teaspoons Worcestershire sauce
8 slices smoked bacon
4 thick slices Emmental cheese
Sliced white onion
Soft lettuce leaves
4 small tomatoes, sliced
Sliced dill pickles
A little butter, softened
4 sesame seed buns, halved lengthwise
Yellow mustard, tomato ketchup and Mayonnaise
(see page 12), to serve

Place the beef, seasoning and Worcestershire sauce in a bowl, and mix well to combine. Divide the mixture into four equal portions. Shape into patties to fit the buns. Cover and leave in a cool place until required. Cook the bacon until crisp, and keep it warm.

Prepare a barbecue, broiler or pan for cooking the burgers. Brush the rack or pan with a little vegetable oil, and cook the burgers, turning once. Cook for 4 minutes on each side for a medium-rare burger, or longer if a more thoroughly cooked burger is required. Just before the burgers are ready, top each one with a slice of cheese and let the cheese melt. Toward the end of cooking, butter the cut sides of the buns, and broil to toast lightly.

To serve, divide the onion, lettuce, tomatoes and dill pickles between the four bottom halves of the buns. Place a burger on each, and top each burger with two slices of crispy bacon and a bun top. Serve the condiments separately. SERVES 4

BACON & BLUE CHEESE BURGERS

1½ pounds medium- or coarse-ground beef
Salt and ground black pepper
4 thick slices Dolcelatte cheese
Sliced plum tomatoes
Soft lettuce leaves
4 ciabatta buns, split lengthwise
Olive oil for brushing
4 slices cooked pancetta (Italian cured "bacon"),
halved

Place the beef and seasoning in a bowl, and mix well to combine. Divide the mixture into four equal portions, and shape into patties.

Prepare a barbecue, broiler or pan for cooking the burgers. Brush the rack or pan with a little oil, and cook the burgers, turning once with a large spatula. Cook for 4 minutes on each side for a medium-rare burger, or longer if a more thoroughly cooked burger is required. Toward the end of cooking, top each burger with a slice of cheese and let the cheese melt. Brush the cut sides of the buns with olive oil, and broil to toast them lightly.

To serve, divide the lettuce and sliced tomatoes between the four bottom halves of the buns. Place a cheeseburger on each, and top each burger with a slice of cooked pancetta. Finish with the bun tops, and serve at once. SERVES 4

TOP: Bacon Cheeseburger
BOTTOM: Bacon & Blue Cheese Burger

BURGERS WITH MUSHROOM TOPPING

1½ pounds lean ground beef
Salt and ground black pepper
I small onion, very finely chopped
4 whole-wheat hamburger buns,
split lengthwise
Chicory lettuce leaves

MUSHROOM TOPPING

⅓ cup butter
3 tablespoons vegetable oil
8 ounces mixed mushrooms, such as brown, field,
oyster and girolles, sliced
Salt and ground black pepper

Place the beef, seasoning and onion in a bowl, and mix well to combine. Divide the mixture into four equal portions, and shape into patties to fit the buns.

Prepare a barbecue, broiler or pan for cooking the burgers. Brush the rack or pan with a little oil, and cook the burgers, turning once. Cook for 4 minutes on each side for a medium-rare burger, or longer if a more thoroughly cooked burger is required.

When the burgers are half-cooked, start cooking the mushroom topping. Heat half the butter and half the oil in a large skillet, and sauté half the mushrooms for about 2 minutes, until lightly cooked. Season well, and keep warm while cooking the second batch of mushrooms.

Toast the whole-wheat buns and place a little lettuce on the four bottom halves of the buns. Place a burger on each bun, top each burger with a quarter of the cooked mushrooms, and finish with the bun tops. Serve at once. SERVES 4

ONION & MUSTARD BURGERS

1½ pounds lean minced beef
Salt and ground black pepper
2 teaspoons dry mustard
4 tablespoons Mayonnaise (see page 12)
4 teaspoons mustard
A little butter, softened
4 floury white buns, split lengthwise

CARAMELIZED ONIONS

2 large onions, sliced into rings
3 tablespoons vegetable oil
2 teaspoons brown sugar

Place the beef and seasoning in a bowl, and mix well to combine. Divide the mixture into four equal portions, and shape into patties.

Prepare the caramelized onions. Heat the oil in a saucepan, and add the onion. Cook over a low heat for about 8-10 minutes, until the onions are really soft. Stir in the brown sugar, and cook for a further 2 minutes. Set aside.

Prepare a barbecue, broiler or pan for cooking the burgers. Brush the rack or pan with a little oil, and cook the burgers, turning once. Cook for 4 minutes on each side for a medium-rare burger, or longer if desired.

Mix together the mayonnaise and mustard, and set aside. Butter the cut sides of the buns sparingly, and broil to toast lightly.

To serve, divide the mayonnaise between the four bottom halves of the buns. Place a burger on each, then top with the caramelized onions and bun tops. Serve immediately. SERVES 4

RIGHT: Burger with Mushroom Topping

CHILI BURGERS

2 tablespoons vegetable oil
I onion, finely chopped
2 cloves garlic, crushed
I tablespoon crushed chili flakes
2 teaspoons ground cumin
1½ pounds ground beef
2 tablespoons sun-dried tomato paste
4 tablespoons chopped fresh cilantro
Salt and ground black pepper
4 wheat tortillas, warmed through
Romaine lettuce leaves, and sliced tomato
and onion, to serve

Heat the oil in a saucepan, and cook the onion and garlic for 3 minutes until soft. Add the crushed chili flakes and cumin, and cook for a further 2 minutes. Set aside to cool.

Place the beef in a bowl. Add the cooked onion mixture, sun-dried tomato paste, cilantro and seasoning, and mix well to combine. Divide the mixture into four equal portions, and shape into patties.

Prepare a barbecue, broiler or pan for cooking the burgers. Brush the rack or pan with a little oil, and cook the burgers, turning once. Cook for 4 minutes on each side for a medium-rare burger, or longer if a more thoroughly cooked burger is required.

Serve each burger in a warm tortilla with lettuce, onion and tomato. SERVES 4

HICKORY BARBECUE BURGERS

1½ pounds ground sirloin steak
I small onion, finely chopped
4 tablespoons good-quality barbecue sauce
2 tablespoons chopped fresh parsley
Salt and ground black pepper
A little butter, softened
4 hamburger buns, split lengthwise
Salad garnish, to include lettuce, tomato and sliced green bell peppers
Sliced dill pickles
Extra barbecue sauce

Place the beef, onion, barbecue sauce, parsley and seasoning in a bowl, and mix well to combine. Divide the mixture into four equal portions, and shape into patties to fit the buns.

Prepare a barbecue, broiler or pan for cooking the burgers. Brush the rack or pan with a little oil, and cook the burgers, turning once. Cook for 4 minutes on each side for a medium-rare burger, or longer if a more thoroughly cooked burger is required. Butter the cut sides of the buns sparingly, and broil to toast them lightly.

To serve, divide the salad garnish between the four bottom halves of the buns. Place a burger on each. Top with dill pickles and the bun tops. Serve at once, passing extra barbecue sauce separately. SERVES 4

TOP: Hickory Barbecue Burger
BOTTOM: Chili Burger

DOUBLE-DECKER BURGERS

HERB BURGERS
1 pound lean ground beef
1 teaspoon mixed dried herbs
Salt and ground black pepper

BEEF AND MUSHROOM BURGERS
¼ cup butter
1⅓ cups chopped mushrooms
1 pound lean ground beef
Salt and ground black pepper

4 whole-wheat hamburger buns, each sliced in three
horizontal layers
Soft lettuce leaves
Yellow mustard
Sliced onion
Tomato Relish (see page 16)

Place the beef, herbs and seasoning for the herb burgers in a bowl, and mix well to combine. Divide the mixture into four equal portions, shape into patties, and set aside.

Prepare the beef and mushroom burgers. Melt the butter in a pan, and sauté the mushrooms for 3-4 minutes. Cool slightly, and then add them to the ground beef and seasoning. Mix well, and shape into four equal-sized patties.

Prepare a barbecue, broiler or pan for cooking the burgers. Brush the rack or pan with a little oil, and cook the burgers, turning once. Cook for 2½ minutes on each side for a medium-rare burger, or longer if desired.

To serve, divide the soft lettuce between the four bun bottoms. Place a mushroom burger on each, and top with the middle bun layers. Place a herb burger on each bun, and top with mustard, onion and Tomato Relish. Finish with the bun tops, and serve. SERVES 4

HAWAIIAN BURGERS

1½ pounds medium- or coarse-ground beef
Salt and ground black pepper
2 tablespoons chopped fresh parsley
4 sesame seed buns, split lengthwise
Mayonnaise (see page 12)
Romaine lettuce leaves
4 slices honey-roast ham
4 slices canned or fresh pineapple

Place the beef, seasoning and parsley in a bowl, and mix well to combine. Divide the mixture into four equal portions, and shape into patties to fit the buns.

Prepare a barbecue, broiler or pan for cooking the burgers. Brush the rack or pan with a little oil, and cook the burgers, turning once. Cook for 4 minutes on each side for a medium-rare burger, or longer if a more thoroughly cooked burger is required. Toast the cut sides of the buns lightly.

To serve, top the four bottom halves of the buns with a dollop of mayonnaise, followed by lettuce leaves and a slice of ham. Place a burger on each, and top with a slice of pineapple. Finish with the bun tops, and serve the burgers at once, passing extra mayonnaise separately. SERVES 4

RIGHT: Hawaiian Burger

FROM THE TURF

The following recipes use a wide variety of meats to create internationally flavored burgers, such as the Chinese Burger. The unusual Croque Monsieur and "Café Parisien" burgers are French-bistro inspired. Along with beef, chicken, pork and lamb, some of the other meats used in this chapter are veal, venison, turkey and sausage.

RIO GRANDE BURGERS

1½ pounds coarse-ground beef
¾ cup finely chopped onion
Salt and ground black pepper
½ teaspoon ground cumin
½ teaspoon ground coriander
2 cloves garlic, crushed
A little butter, softened
4 mixed-grain buns, halved lengthwise
1 large jalapeño chili, thinly sliced
Batavia lettuce leaves
1 onion, sliced into rings
Sweet Pepper Mayonnaise (see page 12)

Place the beef, onion, seasoning, spices and garlic in a bowl, and mix well. Divide into four equal portions, and shape into patties.

Prepare a barbecue, broiler or pan for cooking the burgers. Brush the rack or pan with a little oil, and cook the burgers for 4 minutes on each side for a medium-rare burger, or longer if desired. Toward the end of cooking, butter the cut sides of the buns, and broil to toast.

To serve, divide the chili, lettuce and onion between the four bottom bun halves. Place a burger on each, and top with a spoonful of the mayonnaise. Finish with the bun tops, and serve at once.   SERVES 4

HERBED BEEF PATTIES

1½ pounds coarse-ground beef
4 tablespoons chopped fresh mixed herbs, such as parsley, chives, oregano and thyme
Salt and ground black pepper
Lemon Marinade (see page 10)
8 slices cornbread
Lettuce
Sliced onion
Garlic Mayonnaise (see page 12)
Halved cherry tomatoes, to serve

Place the beef, herbs and seasoning in a bowl, and mix well to combine. Divide the mixture into four equal portions, and shape into patties. Place the patties in a single layer in a glass dish, and pour the marinade over the patties. Cover and chill for at least 2 hours, or, preferably, overnight.

Either barbecue or pan-fry the patties, basting each one well before starting to cook them. Cook for 4 minutes on each side for a medium-rare patty, or longer if a more thoroughly cooked patty is required. Toward the end of cooking, toast the slices of cornbread lightly.

To serve, divide the lettuce and onion between the four slices of bread. Top each with a patty, and spoon on a dollop of Garlic Mayonnaise. Finish with the remaining slices of bread, and serve at once with the halved cherry tomatoes.   SERVES 4

RIGHT: Rio Grande Burger

ITALIAN BURGERS

1½ pounds coarse-ground beef
1 cup finely chopped full-flavored Italian salami
4 tablespoons chopped fresh oregano
Salt and ground black pepper
Mediterranean Marinade (see page 10)
8 ounces mozzarella cheese, cut into 4
4 pieces focaccia bread, halved lengthwise
Oak leaf lettuce
Sliced beef tomatoes
Sliced red onions

Place the beef, salami, oregano and seasoning in a bowl, and mix well to combine. Divide the mixture into four equal portions, and shape into patties. Place the patties in a single layer in a glass dish, and pour the marinade over the patties. Cover and chill for at least 2 hours, or overnight.

Either broil or barbecue the burgers. Cook them for 5 minutes on one side, basting with the reserved marinade, and then turn them over and cook for a further 5 minutes, continuing to baste. Top each burger with a slice of mozzarella for the last 1½ minutes of cooking. These times will produce a medium-rare burger; adjust cooking times to suit personal preference. Toast the cut sides of the focaccia bread lightly.

To serve, divide the lettuce and tomato between the four bottom pieces of bread. Place a burger on each, and top with the red onion slices. Finish with the top slices of bread, and serve immediately. SERVES 4

BEEF, BASIL & TOMATO BURGERS

1½ pounds ground beef
2 tablespoons sun-dried tomatoes in oil, drained and chopped
2 tablespoons shredded fresh basil
4 tablespoons grated Parmesan cheese
Salt and ground black pepper
4 ciabatta buns, halved lengthwise
Olive oil for brushing
Mixed Italian salad leaves
Fresh basil leaves
Sun-dried tomato strips
Mayonnaise (see page 12)

Place the ground beef, sun-dried tomato, basil, Parmesan and seasoning in a bowl, and mix well to combine. Divide the mixture into four equal portions, and shape into patties. Cover the patties and leave in a cool place until required.

These burgers may be broiled, barbecued or pan-fried. Brush the broiler rack or pan with olive oil, and cook the burgers, turning once. Cook for 4 minutes on each side for a medium-rare burger, or longer if a more thoroughly cooked burger is required. Toward the end of cooking, brush the cut sides of the buns with olive oil, and broil to toast lightly.

To serve, place a small amount of the mixed salad leaves on the bottom half of each bun. Place a burger on each, and top with fresh basil, sun-dried tomato strips and a dollop of mayonnaise. Finish with the bun tops, and divide the remaining salad leaves between four plates. SERVES 4

TOP: Italian Burger
BOTTOM: Beef, Basil & Tomato Burger

BOMBAY BURGERS

2 tablespoons vegetable oil
1 onion, finely chopped
5 teaspoons curry powder
1 teaspoon turmeric
1½ pounds ground lamb
3 tablespoons cooked green peas
Salt and ground black pepper
Tandoori Marinade (see page 10)
4 mini naan breads, split lengthwise
Romaine lettuce leaves
Greek-style natural yogurt
Tropical Mango Salsa (see page 14)

Heat the oil in a pan, and cook the onion and spices for 3-4 minutes until soft. Cool this mixture, then add the ground lamb, peas and seasoning, and mix well to combine. Divide the mixture into four equal portions, and shape into patties. Place the patties in a single layer in a glass dish, and pour the marinade over the patties. Cover and chill for at least 2 hours, or overnight.

Pan-fry the burgers; cook them over a fairly low heat for 7 minutes on each side, until they are cooked all the way through. Warm the naan breads.

To serve, divide the lettuce between the four bottom halves of bread. Spoon a dollop of yogurt over each bed of lettuce, and top with a burger. Spoon on some mango salsa, and finish with the naan tops. Serve at once, with extra salsa and yogurt.   SERVES 4

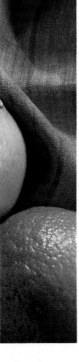

MOROCCAN BURGERS

2 tablespoons olive oil
3 cloves garlic, crushed
2 tablespoons pine nuts
1 tablespoon ground coriander
2 teaspoons ground cumin
1½ pounds ground lamb
4 tablespoons finely chopped dried apricots
Salt and ground black pepper
4 pita breads, split lengthwise
Shredded iceberg lettuce

CUCUMBER AND MINT YOGURT
¾ cup natural yogurt
1 cup peeled and finely diced cucumber
1 tablespoon chopped fresh mint

Heat the oil in a pan, and cook the garlic for 2-3 minutes until soft. Add the pine nuts, and cook for a further minute. Stir in the spices, and cook them briefly. Cool the mixture slightly.

Place the lamb, apricots and seasoning in a bowl. Add the cooled garlic mixture, and mix well to combine. Divide the mixture into four equal portions, and shape into patties.

Prepare a barbecue, broiler or pan for cooking the burgers. Brush the rack or pan with a little oil, and cook the burgers for 6-7 minutes on each side until cooked through.

Mix together the yogurt, cucumber and chopped mint. Warm the pita bread.

To serve, place some lettuce and a burger in each pita pocket, spoon over some yogurt, and serve at once, passing extra yogurt separately.   SERVES 4

RIGHT: Bombay Burger

CHINESE BURGERS

1½ pounds ground pork
3 scallions, finely chopped
1 tablespoon grated fresh ginger root
2 tablespoons soy sauce
16 water chestnuts, finely chopped
Chinese Marinade (see page 10)
8 Chinese pancakes, available from
Oriental supermarkets
Chili sauce, to serve

BEANSPROUT SALAD

1½ cups beansprouts
6 radishes, sliced
½ cucumber, peeled and cut into thin strips
1 green chili, seeded and sliced
3 tablespoons chopped fresh cilantro

Place the pork, scallions, ginger root, soy sauce and water chestnuts in a bowl, and mix well to combine. Divide the mixture into four equal portions, and shape into patties. Place the patties in a single layer in a glass dish, and pour the marinade over the patties. Cover and chill for at least 2 hours, or, preferably, overnight.

Either broil or barbecue these burgers, cooking them for 5-6 minutes on each side, basting with the reserved marinade during cooking.

Place the ingredients for the salad in a bowl, and toss well. Warm the Chinese pancakes.

To serve, place some salad on two pancakes, top with a burger, and fold the pancakes over. Repeat for the remaining burgers. Serve at once, passing the chili sauce separately.   SERVES 4

MARINATED PORK BURGERS

Use quick-cooking polenta or traditional cornmeal in this recipe. Follow the package instructions to cook polenta; then proceed as described in the recipe.

1½ pounds ground pork
4 tablespoons chopped fresh cilantro
2 cloves garlic, crushed
Salt and ground black pepper
Tangy Marinade (see page 10)
4 circles of cooked polenta, cut to fit the burgers
A little olive oil for brushing
Chicory and radicchio leaves, to serve

Place the pork, cilantro, garlic and seasoning in a bowl, and mix well to combine. Divide the mixture into four equal portions, and shape into patties. Place the patties in a single layer in a glass dish, and pour the marinade over the patties. Cover and chill for at least 2 hours, or, preferably, overnight.

Either broil or barbecue the burgers, cooking them for 4 minutes on one side, basting with reserved marinade. Turn them over, baste again, and cook for a further 4 minutes, until cooked through.

Brush the circles of polenta with olive oil, and broil or barbecue them for 3 minutes on each side, until they are pale golden.

To serve, place a burger on each circle of polenta, and serve at once, garnished with the salad leaves.
SERVES 4

TOP: Marinated Pork Burger
BOTTOM: Chinese Burger

SPICY CHICKEN & CORN BURGERS

2 tablespoons olive oil

I onion, finely chopped

2 cloves garlic, crushed

I tablespoon paprika

6 cups ground chicken

I cup canned corn kernels, drained

Salt and ground black pepper

4 hamburger buns, split lengthwise

1¼ cups grated sharp Gouda cheese

Crisp lettuce leaves

Red bell pepper rings

Mayonnaise (see page 12)

Tomato Relish (see page 16), to serve

Heat the oil in a pan, and cook the onion and garlic for 4 minutes until soft. Stir in the paprika, and cook for a further minute. Cool the mixture, and then combine it with the chicken, corn and seasoning. Divide into four portions, and shape into patties.

Prepare a barbecue, broiler or pan for cooking the burgers. Brush the rack or pan with a little oil, and cook the burgers for 5 minutes on each side, until cooked through.

Broil the cut sides of the burger buns to toast lightly. Turn the four tops of the buns over, and sprinkle with the grated Gouda cheese. Broil the cheesy bun tops for a further 1½ minutes, until the cheese is melted.

To serve, divide the lettuce between the four bottom halves of bun, top with red bell pepper rings and the burgers, then spoon on some mayonnaise and finish with the bun tops. Serve at once, accompanied by Tomato Relish. SERVES 4

CHICKEN BURGERS WITH TARRAGON & PROSCIUTTO

2 tablespoons vegetable oil

I red onion, finely chopped

2 cloves garlic, crushed

6 cups ground chicken

Salt and ground black pepper

4 ounces prosciutto, cut into thin strips

2 tablespoons chopped fresh tarragon

A little butter, softened

4 mixed-grain buns, split lengthwise

Lettuce leaves

Marinated artichokes and marinated green olives, to serve

Heat the oil in a pan, and cook the onion and garlic for 3 minutes until soft. Cool the mixture, and place it in a bowl with the chicken and seasoning; mix well to combine. Divide into eight equal portions, and shape into patties. Place a quarter of the prosciutto and tarragon in the center of four of the patties. Place the other four patties over these, and reshape to make four stuffed burgers.

Prepare a barbecue, broiler or pan for cooking the burgers. Brush the rack or pan with a little oil, and cook the burgers for 4½ minutes on each side, until cooked through. Butter the cut sides of the buns, and toast them lightly.

To serve, divide the lettuce between the four bottom halves of bun. Top with burgers and finish with the bun tops. Serve at once with marinated artichokes and olives. SERVES 4

TOP: Spicy Chicken & Corn Burger
BOTTOM: Chicken Burger with Tarragon & Prosciutto

TURKEY, ORANGE & THYME BURGERS

4 cups ground turkey
1 shallot, finely chopped
2 tablespoons chopped fresh thyme
2 tablespoons grated orange zest
Salt and ground black pepper
8 slices sourdough rye bread
Corn salad
Mayonnaise (see page 12)
Cranberry Relish (see page 14)

Place the turkey, shallot, thyme, orange zest and seasoning in a bowl, and mix well to combine. Divide the mixture into four portions, and shape into patties.

Prepare a barbecue, broiler or pan for cooking the burgers. Brush the rack or pan with a little oil, and cook the burgers for 4 minutes on each side, until cooked through. Toast the slices of bread lightly.

To serve, divide the corn salad between four slices of the bread, top with mayonnaise and a burger, and place a spoonful of relish on each burger. Top the burgers with the remaining slices of bread, and serve at once with extra relish and mayonnaise. SERVES 4

TURKEY TIKKA BURGERS

4 cups ground turkey
8 teaspoons tikka paste
4 tablespoons chopped fresh cilantro
Salt and ground black pepper
4 mini naan breads, split lengthwise
Sliced red onion
Romaine lettuce leaves
Lemon wedges, to serve

MINT RAITA
¾ cup natural yogurt
3 tablespoons chopped fresh mint
Pinch of paprika

Place the turkey, tikka paste, cilantro and seasoning in a bowl, and mix well to combine. Divide the mixture into four equal portions, and shape into patties.

Prepare a barbecue, broiler or pan for cooking the burgers. Brush the rack or pan with a little oil, and cook the burgers for 3½ minutes on each side, until cooked through.

Place the ingredients for the raita in a bowl, and mix well to combine.

To serve, divide the onion and lettuce between the four bottom halves of the naan breads, and top each with a burger, followed by a spoonful of raita. Finish with the naan tops, and serve at once with lemon wedges, passing extra raita separately. SERVES 4

RIGHT: Turkey, Orange & Thyme Burger

GREEK BURGERS

4 tablespoons olive oil
I onion, finely chopped
3 cloves garlic, crushed
I pound ground beef
I pound ground lamb
4 tablespoons chopped fresh parsley
24 kalamata olives, pitted and chopped
Salt and ground black pepper
2 cups cubed feta cheese
4 pita breads, split lengthwise
Lettuce leaves
Sliced beef tomatoes
Greek-style pickled green chilies, to serve

Heat half of the oil in a pan, and cook the onion and garlic for 4 minutes until soft. Cool this mixture, and then place in a bowl with the ground meat, parsley, olives and seasoning, and mix well. Divide into four equal portions, and shape into patties.

Brush the burgers with the remaining oil, and broil under a medium-hot broiler for 6 minutes on each side. Two or three minutes before the end of cooking time, divide the cheese cubes between the four burgers, and return to the broiler to cook the cheese until it turns a golden color. (The broiler rack may need to be inverted when cooking the cheese, so it is not so close to the heat.) Warm the pita breads.

To serve, divide the lettuce and tomato between the pita breads, and top each with a burger. Serve with pickled green chilies. SERVES 4

LAMB & HAZELNUT BURGERS WITH GOAT CHEESE

3 tablespoons olive oil
3 shallots, finely chopped
2 cloves garlic, crushed
1½ pounds ground lamb
I tablespoon chopped fresh rosemary
I tablespoon chopped fresh thyme
¼ cup chopped, toasted hazelnuts
Salt and ground black pepper
5 ounces goat cheese, sliced into 4
4 slices olive ciabatta bread or focaccia bread
Continental salad leaves
Sliced plum tomatoes

Heat 2 tablespoons of the oil in a pan, and cook the shallots and garlic for 4 minutes until soft. Cool the mixture, and then place it in a bowl with the lamb, herbs, nuts and seasoning. Mix well, divide into four equal portions, and shape into patties.

Brush the burgers with the remaining oil, and broil under a medium-hot grill for 4½ minutes on each side. Two minutes before the end of the cooking time, place a slice of goat cheese on each burger, and return to the broiler to melt the cheese. (The broiler rack may need to be inverted when cooking the cheese so it is not so close to the heat.) Toast the bread lightly.

To serve, place a burger on each piece of bread, and garnish with the salad leaves and tomato slices.
SERVES 4

TOP: Lamb & Hazelnut Burger
with Goat Cheese
BOTTOM: Greek Burger

VEAL & SAGE BURGERS

⅓ cup dried cèpe mushrooms
4 cups ground veal
2 shallots, finely chopped
1 tablespoon red wine
1 tablespoon chopped fresh sage
Salt and ground black pepper
A little butter, softened
4 pieces French bread, split lengthwise
Green salad and Herb Mayonnaise with sage
(see page 12), to serve

Soak the cèpe mushrooms in hot water for 10 minutes, then drain and chop finely. Place the cèpes in a bowl with the veal, shallots, wine, sage and seasoning, and mix well to combine. Divide the mixture into four equal portions, and shape into patties.

Prepare a barbecue, broiler or pan for cooking the burgers. Brush the rack or pan with a little oil, and cook the burgers for 4 minutes on each side, until cooked through. Butter the cut sides of the French bread, and broil until they are lightly toasted.

To serve, place the burgers between the slices of toasted bread, and serve with green salad and Herb Mayonnaise. SERVES 4

VENISON BURGERS WITH SPICED APPLES

4 cups ground venison
1 tablespoon chopped fresh thyme
1 tablespoon chopped fresh parsley
Salt and ground black pepper
8 slices bacon
2 large red-skinned apples
¼ cup butter
½ teaspoon ground cinnamon
Good pinch of grated nutmeg
4 hamburger buns, split lengthwise
Soft lettuce leaves

Place the venison, herbs and seasoning in a bowl, and mix well to combine. Divide the mixture into four equal portions, and shape into patties. Wrap two slices of bacon around each, and secure with toothpicks.

Broil or barbecue the burgers. Brush the rack with a little oil, and cook the burgers for 6 minutes on each side, until cooked through. Toast the cut sides of the buns lightly.

While the burgers are cooking, prepare the spiced apples. Core the apples, and slice them into thick rings. Heat half the butter in a large pan, and cook half the apple slices for 4-5 minutes until tender. Sprinkle over half the spices, and keep apples warm while cooking the second batch in the remaining butter.

To serve, place some soft lettuce on the bottom halves of the buns, top each with some apple slices and a burger. Finish with the bun tops, and serve at once.
SERVES 4

RIGHT: Venison Burger with Spiced Apples

SANTIAGO BURGERS

4 cups ground pork
I cup finely chopped chorizo sausage
1½ cups mashed cooked chickpeas
½ small green bell pepper, finely chopped
Salt and ground black pepper
8 slices Spanish country bread
Olive oil for brushing
Lettuce leaves
Onion slices and black olives, to serve

Place the pork, chorizo, chickpeas, bell pepper and seasoning in a bowl, and mix well to combine. Divide the mixture into four, and shape into patties.

Prepare a barbecue, broiler or pan for cooking the burgers. Brush the rack or pan with a little vegetable oil, and cook the burgers for 5 minutes on each side, until cooked through. Brush the bread slices with olive oil, and toast them lightly.

To serve, divide the lettuce between four slices of the bread. Top each with a burger and the remaining slices of bread. Serve at once, accompanied by onion slices and black olives. SERVES 4

SATAY BURGERS

5 tablespoons peanut oil
2 shallots, finely chopped
3 cloves garlic, crushed
I teaspoon ground coriander
I teaspoon ground cumin
½ teaspoon turmeric
4 cups ground chicken
8 slices white bread
Cucumber Relish (see page 14), to serve

SPICY PEANUT SAUCE

I tablespoon vegetable oil
I clove garlic, crushed
2 teaspoons crushed dried chilies
2 teaspoons soy sauce
2 tablespoons brown sugar
6 tablespoons crunchy peanut butter
⅔ cup water

Heat I tablespoon of the peanut oil in a pan, and cook the shallot and garlic for 3 minutes until soft. Stir in the spices, and cook for a further minute. Cool the mixture, and then mix it in a bowl with the chicken and seasoning. Divide into four, and shape into patties.

Prepare the peanut sauce. Cook the garlic in the oil over a low heat for 2 minutes. Add the chilies, and cook for a further minute. Stir in the remaining ingredients, and simmer the sauce gently for 3 minutes. Keep warm.

Pan-fry the burgers in the remaining oil, cooking them for 4½ minutes on each side, until cooked through. Toast the bread lightly.

To serve, place each burger between two slices of toast. Serve accompanied by the peanut sauce and Cucumber Relish. SERVES 4

RIGHT: Santiago Burger

BURGERS "CAFE PARISIEN"

4 x 4-ounce entrecôte or rump steaks
Salt and ground black pepper
Olive oil for brushing
4 pieces French baguette, split
Dijon mustard, to taste
Chicory leaves tossed in vinaigrette

Trim the steaks of all fat, and season them well. Brush each steak with olive oil, and broil for about 4½ minutes on each side under a moderately hot broiler. This will produce a medium-rare steak – adjust the cooking times accordingly to suit personal preferences. Toast the French baguette lightly.

To serve, spread mustard on the cut sides of the toasted bread, and sandwich the steaks between the pieces of baguette. Serve at once with the dressed chicory, passing extra mustard if desired. SERVES 4

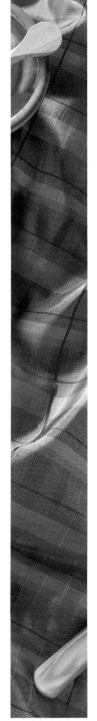

CROQUE-MONSIEUR BISTRO BURGERS

4 x 3-ounce ham steaks
½ cups grated Cantal or Cheddar cheese
4 fried eggs
4 thick slices French country bread
A little butter, softened
Sautéed mushrooms or broiled tomatoes,
to serve (optional)

Grease a large skillet lightly, and cook the ham steaks on one side for 3 minutes. Turn them over, sprinkle with the grated cheese, and continue cooking for a further 3 minutes, until the steaks are cooked and the cheese has begun to melt. Toast the bread lightly.

To serve, butter one side of the toasted bread slices, and place a cheese and ham steak on each slice. Top each steak with a fried egg, and serve at once with sautéed mushrooms or broiled tomatoes, if desired.
SERVES 4

TOP: Croque-Monsieur Bistro Burger
BOTTOM: Burger "Café Parisien"

FROM THE SURF

Fish and seafood form the basic ingredients for the burgers in this chapter. Along with simple Tuna & Corn Burgers are exotic Acapulco Crab Burgers, as well as highly unusual burgers, such as sesame-coated Spicy Thai Fish Patties and sushi-inspired Osaka Fish Cakes.

SALMON & DILL BURGERS

4 cups minced, skinless, boneless salmon
¾ cup mashed potato
4 tablespoons chopped fresh dill
2 tablespoons chopped gherkins
I teaspoon green peppercorns in brine, crushed
Salt to taste
½ cup sunflower oil
4 bagels, split lengthwise
4 tablespoons cream cheese
Watercress sprigs
Sliced dill pickles
Potato Salad (see page 72), to serve

Place the minced salmon, potato, dill, gherkins, peppercorns and salt in a bowl, and mix well. Divide into four, and shape into patties.

Heat the sunflower oil in a large skillet, and cook the burgers over a moderately low heat for 4½ minutes on each side, until cooked through. Toast the bagels lightly.

To serve, spread I tablespoon of cream cheese on the bottom half of each bagel, top with some watercress and a burger. Finish with sliced dill pickles and the bagel tops. Serve at once, accompanied by Potato Salad. SERVES 4

POTATO LATKES

4 medium baking potatoes, peeled and grated
4 small shallots, finely chopped
I beaten egg
Salt and ground black pepper
¾ cup olive oil
4 slices light rye bread
4 tablespoons sour cream
4 teaspoons snipped fresh chives
4 teaspoons salmon caviar or cod's roe
4 ounces salmon lox, cut into strips
Salad garnish of chicory, radicchio and endive

Squeeze the moisture out of the grated potatoes so they are as dry as possible. Place them in a bowl with the shallots, beaten egg and seasoning. Mix thoroughly to combine, and divide the mixture into four patties.

Heat half the oil in a large skillet, and cook two of the latkes over a medium-low heat for 5 minutes on each side, until golden and cooked through. Remove, and drain on paper towels. Repeat with the remaining oil and latkes. Toast the rye bread lightly.

To serve, place a latke on each slice of toasted rye bread, and top each one with a quarter of the sour cream, chives, caviar or cod's roe and lox. Garnish with the mixed salad leaves, and serve at once.
SERVES 4

RIGHT: Salmon & Dill Burger

48

LOCH FYNE BURGERS

4 cups minced skinless kippered herring

1¼ cups mashed potato

2 teaspoons horseradish

4 teaspoons chopped fresh chervil

Ground black pepper

¾ cup coarse oatmeal

½ cup sunflower oil

4 Staffordshire oatcakes (thin oatmeal pancakes),
warmed through

Sliced tomatoes

Mixed salad leaves

HORSERADISH MAYONNAISE

5 tablespoons Mayonnaise (see page 12)

2 teaspoons horseradish

Place the minced kippered herrings, potato, horseradish, chervil and pepper in a bowl, and mix well to combine. (These burgers do not need salt, as the kippered herrings are very salty.) Divide the mixture into four equal portions, and shape into patties. Roll the patties in the oatmeal to coat thoroughly.

Heat the sunflower oil in a large skillet, and cook the burgers over a moderately low heat for 5 minutes on each side, until cooked through.

Make the horseradish mayonnaise by mixing the ingredients thoroughly.

To serve, place each burger in an oatcake, topped with a slice of tomato and a few mixed salad leaves. Pass the horseradish mayonnaise separately.

SERVES 4

ENGLISH FISH CAKES

1 onion, finely chopped

2 tablespoons vegetable oil

4 cups minced skinless, boneless haddock

1¼ cups mashed potato

4 teaspoons chopped fresh parsley

Grated zest of 1 lemon

4 teaspoons lemon juice

Salt and ground black pepper

1 beaten egg

1 cup dried breadcrumbs

Vegetable oil for deep-frying

4 English muffins, split lengthwise

A little butter, softened

Soft lettuce leaves

Sliced shallot

Tartar sauce

Heat 2 tablespoons of the oil in a saucepan, and sauté the onion for 3 minutes until soft. Cool and add to the haddock, potato, parsley, lemon zest and juice and seasoning, and mix well to combine. Divide the mixture into four equal portions, and shape into patties.

Dip a fish cake into the beaten egg, and then in the breadcrumbs to coat thoroughly. Repeat with the remaining fish cakes.

Heat the oil for deep-frying. (It is hot enough when a cube of bread, dropped into the oil, floats and bubbles at the surface.) Fry the fish cakes in batches, if necessary, for 6 minutes, until cooked through. Remove, and drain on paper towels. Toast the cut sides of the muffins lightly, and butter them sparingly.

To serve, divide the lettuce and shallot between the four bottom halves of the English muffins, top with a fish cake, a spoonful of tartar sauce and the muffin tops. Serve at once.

SERVES 4

TOP: English Fish Cake
BOTTOM: Loch Fyne Burger

ACAPULCO CRAB BURGERS

3 cups white crabmeat
1¼ cups mashed potato
4 teaspoons chopped fresh cilantro
1 teaspoon chopped fresh red chili
½ teaspoon grated lime zest
2 teaspoons freshly squeezed lime juice
Salt and ground black pepper
1 beaten egg
1½ cups fresh white breadcrumbs
Vegetable oil for deep-frying
4 mixed-grain buns, split lengthwise
A little butter, softened
Lettuce leaves
Tangy Tomato Salsa (see page 14)
Herb Mayonnaise, with cilantro (see page 12)

Squeeze any excess moisture from the crabmeat, and place in a bowl with the potato, cilantro, chili, lime zest and juice, and seasoning. Mix well to combine. Divide into four equal portions, and shape into patties.

Dip a burger into the egg, and then in breadcrumbs to coat well. Repeat with the remaining burgers.

Heat the oil for deep-frying. (It is hot enough when a cube of bread, dropped into the oil, floats and bubbles at the surface.) Deep-fry over a medium-low heat for 10 minutes, until golden and cooked through. Remove, and drain on paper towels. Toast the cut sides of the buns, and butter sparingly.

To serve, divide the lettuce between the four bottom halves of bun. Top with a burger and a spoonful of tomato salsa and herb mayonnaise, and finish with the bun tops. Serve the remaining salsa separately.

SERVES 4

OSAKA FISH CAKES

1½ tablespoons dried arame seaweed, soaked in
2½ cups water for 1 hour
1 teaspoon wasabi powder
1 teaspoon water
1 tablespoon tamari soy sauce
1 tablespoon sunflower oil
1 teaspoon sesame oil
2 teaspoons mirin
¾ cup cooked white rice
8 ounces smoked tuna
8 strips Japanese pink pickled ginger
8 Japanese rice cakes

CUCUMBER AND RADISH SALAD
½ cucumber, peeled and cut into matchsticks
8 radishes, sliced and cut into matchsticks
1 tablespoon rice wine vinegar
½ teaspoon superfine sugar

Drain the soaked arame, and lay it on paper towels to absorb excess moisture. Place the wasabi powder, water and soy sauce in a small bowl, and mix. Heat the two oils in a skillet, add the arame and wasabi mixture, and cook gently for 2 minutes. Let cool.

Mix the mirin into the cooked rice. Divide the smoked tuna into four equal portions, and lay flat on a board. Divide the rice between the tuna, spreading in a thin layer. Divide the arame between the portions, and spread over. Lay two strips of pickled ginger down the center of each pile, and roll the rice portions up. Place the salad ingredients in a bowl and toss.

To serve, slice each sushi roll in half, on the diagonal, and place a cut roll on each rice cake. Serve each person two sushi rolls and rice cakes, accompanied by the cucumber salad.

SERVES 4

RIGHT: Acapulco Crab Burger

SPICY THAI FISH PATTIES

4 cups minced, skinless, boneless cod
1¾ cups minced, cooked, shelled shrimp
4 scallions, finely chopped
2 teaspoons grated fresh ginger root
1 teaspoon finely chopped lime leaves
Salt and ground black pepper
1 beaten egg
1¼ cups white sesame seeds
Vegetable oil for deep-frying
4 slices white bread, crusts removed
Salad garnish of romaine lettuce, cilantro, sliced chili and cucumber
Thai sweet chili sauce, to serve

Place the cod, shrimp, scallions, ginger root, lime leaves and seasoning in a bowl, and mix well to combine. Divide the mixture into eight equal portions, and shape into patties.

Dip a patty into the egg, and then in the sesame seeds to coat. Repeat with the remaining patties.

Heat the oil for deep-frying. (It is hot enough when a cube of bread, dropped into the oil, floats and bubbles at the surface.) Deep-fry the patties over a medium-low heat, in batches if necessary, for 8 minutes, until golden and cooked through. Remove with a slotted spoon, and drain on paper towels. Deep-fry the bread in the hot oil for a few minutes, until pale golden. Remove, and drain on paper towels.

To serve, place two fish patties on each piece of fried bread, and garnish with the salad. Pass the Thai sweet chili sauce separately.   SERVES 4

VALENCIA BURGERS

2 cups minced, skinless, boneless cod
1¾ cups minced, cooked, shelled shrimp
½ cup finely chopped clams
1 shallot, finely chopped
½ teaspoon chopped saffron, infused in 1 tablespoon hot water for 10 minutes
Salt and ground black pepper
Vegetable oil for deep-frying
4 chunks ciabatta bread, split lengthwise
A little olive oil for brushing
Lettuce leaves
Sliced tomato
Sliced orange bell pepper

LEMON AIOLI
4 tablespoons Mayonnaise (see page 12)
1 clove garlic, crushed
Grated zest of 1 lemon
4 teaspoons lemon juice

Place the cod, shrimp, clams, shallot, infused saffron and seasoning in a bowl, and mix well. Divide into four, and shape into patties.

Place the ingredients for the lemon aïoli in a small bowl, and mix to combine. Chill.

Heat the oil for deep-frying. Fry the burgers over a medium-low heat for about 9-10 minutes, until cooked through. Remove, and drain on paper towels. Brush the cut sides of the bread with olive oil, and broil to toast lightly.

To serve, divide the lettuce, sliced tomato and bell pepper between the four bottom halves of bun. Top each with a burger, a spoonful of aïoli and a bun top. Serve at once.   SERVES 4

TOP: Valencia Burger
BOTTOM: Spicy Thai Fish Patties

TUNA & CORN BURGERS

2 cups canned tuna, drained
¾ cup canned corn kernels, drained
I small onion, finely chopped
½ small red bell pepper, finely chopped
4 cups fresh white breadcrumbs
I tablespoon chopped fresh parsley
Salt and ground black pepper
I beaten egg
Vegetable oil for deep-frying
4 hamburger buns, split lengthwise
Crisp lettuce leaves
Coleslaw (see page 72), to serve

Place the tuna in a bowl, and mash it really thoroughly until no large lumps remain. Add the corn, onion, red bell pepper, half the breadcrumbs, parsley and seasoning, and mix well to combine. Divide the mixture into four equal portions, and shape into patties.

Dip each burger into the beaten egg, and then in the remaining breadcrumbs to coat well.

Heat the oil for deep-frying. (It is hot enough when a cube of bread, dropped into the oil, floats and bubbles at the surface.) Fry the burgers in batches, if necessary, for 6 minutes, until golden and warmed through. Remove with a slotted spoon, and drain on paper towels. Toast the buns lightly.

To serve, divide the lettuce between the four bottom halves of the buns, top each with a burger and finish with the bun tops. Serve at once with a helping of Coleslaw on each plate.   SERVES 4

KEDGEREE PATTIES

3 cups minced, skinless, boneless smoked haddock
⅔ cup cooked rice
4 scallions, finely chopped
2 teaspoons chopped fresh parsley
Freshly grated nutmeg
Ground black pepper
½ cup sunflower oil
4 soda bread buns, split lengthwise
A little butter, softened
Crisp lettuce leaves
Sliced tomato

EGG AND CAYENNE MAYONNAISE
2 hard-boiled eggs, peeled and chopped
4 tablespoons Mayonnaise (see page 12)
2 teaspoons cayenne pepper

Place the haddock, rice, scallion, parsley, nutmeg and pepper in a bowl, and mix well. Divide into four, and shape into patties.

Place the ingredients for the egg mayonnaise in a small bowl, and mix to combine. Chill.

Heat the sunflower oil in a large skillet, and cook the patties over a low heat for 5 minutes on each side, until golden and cooked through. Alternatively, cook the patties on a barbecue, on an oiled rack, for about 4-5 minutes on each side. Toast the cut sides of the soda bread buns, and butter them lightly.

To serve, divide the lettuce and tomato between the four bottom halves of the buns. Top each with a patty and a spoonful of mayonnaise, and finish with the tops of the buns. Serve at once, passing extra mayonnaise separately.   SERVES 4

RIGHT: Tuna & Corn Burger

MEATLESS WONDERS

The following vegetarian recipes use ingredients such as potato, pumpkin, parsnip, rice, chickpeas, nuts, bulghur wheat, and beans and lentils to make a firm burger. Breadcrumbs and egg are used to bind the patties in many of the recipes, and most of the burgers benefit from an hour's refrigeration prior to cooking to help hold them together.

ROSTI BURGERS

1½ cups peeled and grated potato
1½ cups grated zucchini
I small red onion, peeled and grated
I cup grated Gruyère cheese
I beaten egg
Salt and ground black pepper
¾ cup vegetable oil
4 mixed-grain buns, split lengthwise
A little butter, softened
Soft lettuce leaves
Tomato Relish (see page 16)

Squeeze out all the excess moisture from the potatoes and zucchini. Place in a bowl with the onion, cheese, egg and seasoning. Mix well, and divide into four. Shape into patties.

Heat the oil in a large pan, and cook two burgers over a medium-low heat for 5 minutes on each side, until crisp. Cook the remaining burgers. Toast the cut sides of the buns, and butter lightly.

To serve, divide the lettuce leaves between the four bottom bun halves, and top each with a burger, a spoonful of relish and a bun top. Serve at once.

SERVES 4

ROOT BURGERS

3 cups parsnip purée (steam parsnips before puréeing)
I cup grated carrot
4 scallions, thinly sliced
Salt and ground black pepper
1¼ cups sunflower seeds
¾ cup sunflower oil
4 floury hamburger buns, split lengthwise
A little butter, softened
Romaine lettuce leaves

TANGY DRESSING
½ cup crème fraîche
4 teaspoons snipped fresh chives
Grated zest of I small orange

Place the parsnip purée, carrot, scallion and seasoning in a bowl, and mix well. Divide the vegetable mixture into four equal portions, and shape into patties. Coat each patty in sunflower seeds, and chill for at least I hour before cooking.

Place the ingredients for the dressing in a bowl, and mix to combine. Chill until needed.

Heat the oil in a large skillet, and cook the burgers over a medium-low heat for 5 minutes on each side, until golden and cooked through. Toast the cut sides of the buns, and butter them sparingly.

To serve, divide the lettuce between the four bottom halves of the buns, and top each with a burger. Finish with the bun tops, and serve at once with the dressing.

SERVES 4

RIGHT: Rosti Burger

RICE & SPINACH BURGERS

1¼ cups cooked mixed long-grain rice
and wild rice
2 cups cooked fresh spinach, squeezed of all
excess moisture
½ red bell pepper, chopped
1 cup grated Cheddar cheese
1 beaten egg
Salt and ground black pepper
A good pinch freshly grated nutmeg
¾ cup dried white breadcrumbs
4 tablespoons grated Parmesan cheese
¾ cup vegetable oil
A little butter, softened
8 slices light rye bread
Sliced tomato
Lettuce leaves and sliced onion, to serve

Place the rice, spinach, red bell pepper, cheese, egg and seasoning in a food processor, and process briefly to combine. Divide the mixture into four equal portions, and shape into patties. Mix together the dried breadcrumbs and Parmesan cheese, and coat the burgers with this mixture. Chill the burgers for at least 1 hour before cooking them.

Heat the oil in a large skillet, and cook the burgers over a medium-low heat for 5 minutes on each side, until cooked through.

To serve, butter one side of each piece of bread. Divide the tomato slices between four slices of the bread, top each with a burger, and finish with the remaining bread. Serve the burgers garnished with the lettuce leaves and sliced onions.   SERVES 4

SPICED PUMPKIN BURGERS

4 cups mashed pumpkin (steam pumpkin
before mashing)
2 shallots, finely chopped
½ red bell pepper, finely chopped
½ green bell pepper, finely chopped
4 tablespoons golden raisins
⅔ cup cooked rice
Salt and ground black pepper
1¼ cups pumpkin seeds
¾ cups olive oil
4 slices cornbread
Olive oil for brushing
Mixed green salad leaves
Mayonnaise (see page 12), to serve

Place the mashed pumpkin, shallots, bell peppers, golden raisins, rice and seasoning in a bowl, and mix well to combine. Divide the mixture into four equal portions, and shape into patties. Coat each patty in pumpkin seeds, and chill the patties for at least 1 hour before cooking.

These burgers are very soft and fragile, and they need to be cooked over a very low heat so the pumpkin seeds do not burn. Heat the oil in a large pan, and cook the burgers very gently for 4-5 minutes on each side, until golden and cooked through. Brush the cornbread with olive oil, and toast it lightly.

To serve, divide the salad leaves between the four slices of bread, and top each with a burger. Serve at once with the mayonnaise.   SERVES 4

TOP: Spiced Pumpkin Burger
BOTTOM: Rice & Spinach Burger

EGGPLANT CHEESE PARCELS

1 large eggplant
3 tablespoons extra virgin olive oil
Salt and ground black pepper
2 ripe plum tomatoes
4 ounces mozzarella cheese
2 tablespoons chopped fresh basil
4 tablespoons extra virgin olive oil
4 chunks ciabatta bread, split lengthwise

Preheat the oven to 350°F. Remove the stalk from the eggplant and slice it lengthwise into four long slices, discarding the two outer edges – you should be left with four flat pieces. Brush each piece on both sides with the 3 tablespoons of olive oil, and season well. Broil the eggplant slices under a moderate broiler for 5 minutes on each side, until pale golden and soft.

Slice each tomato into four, and cut the mozzarella into four thick slices. Mix together the basil and the 4 tablespoons of oil, and use this to brush the cut sides of the bread.

Layer the tomato and mozzarella to produce four stacks, each consisting of one piece of cheese sandwiched between two slices of tomato. Wrap a slice of eggplant around each cheese and tomato stack, and place each parcel between two slices of ciabatta bread. Bake the cheese and bread parcels in the oven for 10 minutes, until the bread is warmed through and the cheese has begun to melt. Serve at once.   SERVES 4

MUSHROOM BURGERS

1½ pounds mixed mushrooms
¾ cup olive oil
¼ cup butter
4 shallots, finely chopped
1 tablespoon chopped fresh thyme
1 tablespoon Madeira
4 cups fresh white breadcrumbs
Salt and ground black pepper
6 hamburger buns, split lengthwise
A little butter, softened
Lettuce leaves
Sliced onion
Sliced tomato
Herb Mayonnaise (see page 12), to serve

Place the mushrooms in a food processor, and process briefly until chopped. Heat 4 tablespoons of the oil and all the butter in a large skillet, and sauté the shallots for 2 minutes. Add the mushrooms, and sauté for a further 4 minutes. Cool the mixture, then stir in the thyme, Madeira, breadcrumbs and seasoning, and mix well. Divide into six portions, and shape into patties. Chill for at least 1 hour.

Heat half the remaining oil in a large skillet, and cook the burgers in two batches over a medium-low heat for 5 minutes on each side, until golden and cooked through. Toast the cut sides of the buns, and butter sparingly.

To serve, divide the lettuce and onion between the six bottom halves of the buns, top each with a burger, some sliced tomato and a bun top. Serve at once, passing Herb Mayonnaise separately.   SERVES 6

RIGHT: Eggplant Cheese Parcel

FALAFEL BURGERS

2½ cups cooked chickpeas
½ cup light tahini
4 tablespoons freshly squeezed lemon juice
4 tablespoons chopped fresh parsley
1 teaspoon ground cumin
2 teaspoons ground coriander
½ teaspoon turmeric
Salt and ground black pepper
¾ cup whole-wheat flour
¾ cup vegetable oil
4 pita breads, warmed and split lengthwise
Lettuce leaves
Sliced tomato
Sliced red onion
Garlic Mayonnaise (see page 12)
Lemon wedges, to serve

Place the chickpeas in a food processor, and process briefly. Add the tahini, lemon juice, parsley, spices and seasoning, and process again until well combined. Divide the mixture into four equal portions, and shape into patties. Roll each patty in whole-wheat flour to coat, and chill for at least 1 hour before cooking.

Heat the oil in a large skillet, and cook the burgers over a medium-low heat for 5 minutes on each side, until golden and cooked through.

To serve, fill each pita bread with lettuce, tomato and onion, and top with a burger and a spoonful of mayonnaise. Serve at once with lemon wedges, passing extra mayonnaise separately.   SERVES 4

LEBANESE BURGERS

2 cups prepared bulghur wheat
1¾ cups cooked cannellini beans
1 clove garlic, crushed
4 tablespoons chopped fresh parsley
2 tablespoons chopped fresh mint
Salt and ground black pepper
¾ cup vegetable oil
4 pita breads, warmed and split lengthwise
Soft lettuce leaves
Halved cherry tomatoes and marinated black olives, to serve

YOGURT DRESSING
6 teaspoons natural yogurt
4 teaspoons chopped fresh parsley
1 teaspoon chopped fresh mint
2 teaspoons lemon juice
1 clove garlic, crushed

Place the bulghur wheat, cannellini beans, garlic, herbs and seasoning in a food processor, and process briefly until combined. Divide the mixture into four equal portions, and shape into patties. Chill for at least 1 hour before cooking.

Place the ingredients for the dressing in a bowl, and mix together to combine. Chill until needed to let the flavors develop.

Heat the oil in a large skillet, and cook the burgers over a low heat for 6 minutes on each side, until golden and cooked through.

To serve, place lettuce leaves and a burger in each pita pocket, and top with a spoonful of dressing. Serve at once with cherry tomatoes and black olives.

SERVES 4

TOP: Lebanese Burger
BOTTOM: Falafel Burger

POLENTA & MUSHROOM BURGERS

Either use quick-cooking polenta or traditional cornmeal for these burgers. Follow the package instructions to cook polenta, and then stamp out circles from the prepared slab as instructed below.

6 tablespoons extra virgin olive oil
4 x 4-inch circles of cooked polenta, about
½ inch thick
Mixed salad leaves tossed in vinaigrette,
to serve

WILD MUSHROOM TOPPING
12 ounces wild mushrooms
⅓ cup butter
3 shallots, sliced
Salt and ground black pepper
2 teaspoons lemon juice
2 tablespoons chopped fresh parsley
2 tablespoons snipped fresh chives

Heat half the oil in a large skillet, and cook two polenta circles over a moderate heat for about 7 minutes on each side, until the polenta is golden on the outside and warmed through. Repeat with the remaining oil and polenta, and keep warm.

To make the mushroom topping, clean the mushrooms, and slice any that are large. Heat half the butter in a large skillet and sauté half the shallots for 2 minutes. Add half the mushrooms, and sauté for 2 minutes. Season well, and stir in half the lemon juice and herbs. Keep warm while cooking the second batch of mushrooms.

To serve, top each polenta burger with a quarter of the mushroom topping, and serve at once with the salad garnish. SERVES 4

PUTTANESCA BURGERS

2¼ cups mashed, cooked green lentils
4 tablespoons sun-dried tomato paste
4 teaspoons chopped capers
2 tablespoons chopped black olives
2 teaspoons chili powder
Salt and ground black pepper
1 cup dried white breadcrumbs
¾ cup olive oil
4 chunks focaccia bread, split lengthwise
Olive oil for brushing
Lettuce leaves
Sliced shallot
Pickled sweet cherry peppers, to serve

Place the lentils, tomato paste, capers, olives, chili powder and seasoning in a bowl, and mix well to combine. Divide the mixture into four equal portions, and shape into patties. Roll the patties in the breadcrumbs to coat. Chill for at least 1 hour.

Heat the oil in a large skillet, and cook the burgers over a medium-low heat for 5 minutes on each side, until golden and cooked through. Brush the cut sides of the focaccia bread with olive oil, and toast lightly.

To serve, divide the lettuce and shallot slices between the four bottom halves of the bread, top with burgers and the bread tops. Serve at once with cherry peppers. SERVES 4

RIGHT: Polenta & Mushroom Burger

VEGETARIAN CHILI BURGERS

2½ cups cooked red kidney beans
1¼ cups cooked black-eyed peas
2 teaspoons cayenne pepper
1 teaspoon ground cumin
½ fresh green chili, finely chopped
Salt and ground black pepper
1 beaten egg
2 cups coarsely crushed tortilla chips
¾ cup vegetable oil
8 slices cornbread
Crisp lettuce
Chili Mayonnaise (see page 12)
Pickled jalapeño chilies, to serve

Place the beans, peas, spices, green chili and seasoning in a food processor, and process until mixture is combined but the beans are still fairly coarse. Divide the mixture into four equal portions, and shape into patties. Dip each patty into egg, and then coat in crushed tortilla chips. Chill for at least 1 hour before cooking.

Heat the oil in a large skillet, and cook the burgers over a medium-low heat for 5 minutes on each side, until golden and cooked. Toast the cornbread lightly.

To serve, divide the lettuce between four slices of the bread. Top each with a burger, followed by a spoonful of Chili Mayonnaise, and finish with the remaining bread. Serve at once with the pickled jalapeño chilies. SERVES 4

THREE-NUT BURGERS

2½ cups chopped raw cashew nuts
1½ cups walnut pieces
2 cups grated red cheese
2 cups fresh white breadcrumbs
2 tablespoons snipped fresh chives
2 eggs
Salt and ground black pepper
1½ cups coarsely crushed, slivered almonds
Oil for deep-frying
8 whole-wheat buns, split lengthwise
Mixed salad leaves
Pumpkin Relish (see page 16), to serve

Place the nuts, cheese, breadcrumbs, chives, one beaten egg and seasoning in a food processor, and process until combined. Divide the mixture into eight equal portions, and shape into patties. Dip each patty into the second beaten egg, and then coat in silvered almonds. Chill for at least 1 hour before cooking.

Heat the oil for deep-frying. (It is hot enough when a cube of bread, dropped into the oil, floats and bubbles at the surface.) Fry the burgers in batches for 7-8 minutes, until golden and cooked through. Remove with a slotted spoon, and drain on paper towels. Toast the buns lightly.

To serve, divide the salad leaves between the bottom halves of the buns. Top each with a burger, and finish with the bun tops. Serve at once with Pumpkin Relish passed separately. SERVES 8

TOP: Three-Nut Burger
BOTTOM: Vegetarian Chili Burger

SIDE ORDERS

Accompaniments to burgers make the meal complete, and the recipes in this chapter are suggestions you may like to try. Along with salads, there are fries made from potatoes and sweet potatoes, as well as vegetable chips made from red beets and carrots. Of course, the simplest accompaniments are ones you may have at home, such as dill pickles and olives, which complement the heartiness of burgers made with meat.

ITALIAN SALAD

4 celery stalks, sliced on the diagonal
1 small red bell pepper, cut into diamonds
1 small green bell pepper, cut into diamonds
2 tablespoons coarsely chopped, flat-leafed Italian parsley
9 black olives and 9 green olives

DRESSING
6 tablespoons extra virgin olive oil
2 tablespoons red wine vinegar
1 teaspoon lightly crushed fennel seeds
1 clove garlic, crushed
Pinch of superfine sugar
Salt and ground black pepper

Place the salad ingredients in a bowl. Place the ingredients for the dressing in a screw-topped jar, and shake well to combine. Taste and adjust seasoning.

Pour the dressing over the salad, and toss well to combine. Cover the salad, and chill for 30 minutes before serving to let the flavors develop.

SERVES 6

ARTICHOKE SALAD WITH BLUE CHEESE DRESSING

14 ounces canned artichoke hearts in brine, drained and halved
½ small iceberg lettuce, torn into bite-sized pieces
12 cherry tomatoes, halved
2 tablespoons snipped fresh chives

BLUE CHEESE DRESSING
½ cup mashed Dolcelatte cheese
Pinch of superfine sugar
Pinch of cayenne pepper
Salt and ground black pepper
6 tablespoons sunflower oil
2 tablespoons white wine vinegar
2 tablespoons sour cream

Divide the prepared salad ingredients between four individual bowls, and set aside until required.

Place the cheese in a food processor with the sugar, cayenne and seasoning, and process briefly to form a smooth paste. Add the oil in a steady stream, with the processor running, to produce a creamy-textured mixture. Add the vinegar and sour cream, and process again briefly until combined. Taste and adjust seasoning, if necessary.

Spoon some dressing over each salad, and serve, passing extra dressing separately.   SERVES 4

TOP: Italian Salad
BOTTOM: Artichoke Salad with Blue Cheese Dressing

POTATO SALAD

1 pound new potatoes
6 tablespoons Mayonnaise (see page 12)
4 tablespoons thick natural yogurt
Salt and ground black pepper
2 scallions, thinly sliced

Scrub or peel the potatoes, and cut them into bite-sized chunks. Cook them for about 5 minutes in boiling, salted water, until they are just tender. Drain and refresh in cold water.

Mix together the mayonnaise, yogurt and seasoning. Fold this mixture into the cooked potatoes, together with scallions. Cover the salad, and chill until required. SERVES 4-6

COLESLAW

½ small white cabbage, finely shredded
¾ cup peeled and grated carrot
2 scallions, sliced into long, thin strips
1 red-skinned apple, cut into matchsticks
5 tablespoons Mayonnaise (see page 12)
4 tablespoons Greek-style yogurt
Salt and ground black pepper

Place the prepared vegetables and the apple in a mixing bowl. Mix together the mayonnaise and yogurt, and season well.

Stir the mayonnaise mixture into the prepared vegetables, and toss gently to coat. Cover the coleslaw, and chill until required. SERVES 6

TOP: Potato Salad
BOTTOM: Coleslaw

FRENCH FRIES

1 6-ounce baking potato per person
Vegetable oil for deep-frying
Salt for sprinkling

Old or baking potatoes will produce the best results. Peel the required quantity of potatoes, and cut them into ½-inch wide strips.

Pour oil into a pan to a depth of about 3 inches. Using a cooking thermometer, heat until the oil reaches a temperature of 250°F – this is a fairly low heat. Alternatively, use a deep-fat fryer, following the manufacturer's cooking instructions.

Cook the potatoes, in batches if necessary, for 9 minutes, until they are partially cooked but are still very pale. Remove the potatoes from the oil with a slotted spoon, and drain on paper towels.

Just before serving, heat the oil to 300°F, and return the potatoes to the oil. Cook them in batches for about 10 minutes, until crisp and golden. Remove the potatoes from the oil, and drain on paper towels. Sprinkle with salt, and serve at once.

GRATED CHILI FRIES

2 ounces baking potatoes per person
Vegetable oil for deep-frying
½ teaspoon chili powder
Pinch of dried chili flakes
1 tablespoon crushed sea salt

Coarsely grate the potatoes, or cut them into julienne strips. Squeeze the potato of all excess moisture, and pat it dry on paper towels.

Pour oil into a pan to a depth of about 3 inches. Heat until a cube of bread, dropped into the oil, floats and bubbles on the surface. Alternatively, test the oil with a thermometer; when it reaches 375°F, it is hot enough. Fry the potatoes, in batches if necessary, for a

few seconds, until pale golden and crisp. Remove the potatoes with a slotted spoon, and drain on paper towels.

Mix the chili powder, flakes and salt together, and sprinkle on the fries.

SWEET POTATO FRIES

6 ounces sweet potatoes per person
Vegetable oil for deep-frying
Salt for sprinkling

Peel the required quantity of sweet potatoes, and cut them into ½-inch wide strips.

Pour oil into a pan to a depth of about 3 inches. Using a cooking thermometer, heat until the oil reaches a temperature of 250°F – this is a fairly low heat. Cook the sweet potatoes, in batches if necessary, for 9 minutes, until they are partially cooked but are still pale. Remove from the oil with a slotted spoon, and drain on paper towels.

Just before serving, heat the oil to 300°F and return the potatoes to the oil. Cook them for about 3 minutes, until crisp and golden. Remove the potatoes from the oil with a slotted spoon, and drain on paper towels. Sprinkle with salt, and serve at once.

TOP TO BOTTOM: Sweet Potato Fries, Grated Chili Fries, French Fries

VEGETABLE CHIPS

The recipes below describe how to make parsnip, carrot, red beet and potato chips. Choose your own combination, or cook a mixture of them all.

PARSNIP CHIPS

2 ounces parsnips per person
Oil for deep-frying
Salt for sprinkling

Peel the parsnips, and slice them very, very thinly. The ideal way of doing this is to use a mandoline. Place the sliced parsnips on paper towels, and pat to remove all excess moisture.

Pour oil into a pan to a depth of 3 inches. Test with a thermometer; when it reaches 375°F, it is hot enough.

Fry the chips, in batches if necessary, for 1½ minutes, until crisp and golden. Remove the chips with a slotted spoon, and drain on paper towels. Sprinkle with salt, and serve at once, or store in an airtight container until required.

CARROT CHIPS

3 ounces carrots per person
Oil for deep-frying
Salt for sprinkling

Follow the instructions for Parsnip Chips, above, except heat the oil to the slightly lower temperature of 350°F.

RED BEET CHIPS

3 ounces red beets per person
Oil for deep-frying
Salt for sprinkling

Follow the instructions for Parsnip Chips, above, except heat the oil to the slightly lower temperature of 350°F, and fry the chips for the longer time of 3 minutes.

POTATO CHIPS

2 ounces potatoes per person
Oil for deep-frying
Salt for sprinkling

These chips need to be double-fried to make them extra crisp. Follow the instructions for Parsnip Chips, left, up to the point where the chips are drained on paper towels. Reheat the oil to 375°F, and re-fry the chips for a further 1½ minutes, until crisp and dark golden. Remove from the oil with a slotted spoon, and drain again on fresh paper towels. Sprinkle with salt before serving.

FRIED GREEN TOMATOES

2 tablespoons all-purpose flour
Salt and ground pepper
1 teaspoon cayenne pepper
4 firm green tomatoes, thickly sliced
¼ cup butter
1 tablespoon chopped fresh parsley

Mix together the flour, seasoning and cayenne pepper. Toss the tomato slices in the flour mixture.

Melt the butter in a large skillet, and cook the tomatoes for 3 minutes on each side. Stir in the parsley, and cook the tomatoes for a further 3 minutes, until they are tender. Serve at once.   SERVES 4

CLOCKWISE: Potato Chips, Assorted Vegetable Chips, Green Fried Tomatoes

POTATO SKINS WITH SOUR CREAM DRESSING

4 large baking potatoes, weighing about
8 ounces each
Oil for deep-frying

SOUR CREAM DRESSING
⅔ cup sour cream
4 tablespoons snipped fresh chives
½ teaspoon lemon juice
Pinch of cayenne pepper
Salt and ground black pepper

Preheat the oven to 400°F. Wash the potatoes, and place them on a baking sheet. Bake in the oven for 40-45 minutes, until they are just cooked. Remove the potatoes from the oven, and let cool.

Meanwhile, prepare the dressing. Place the sour cream, chives, lemon juice, cayenne pepper and seasoning in a bowl, and mix thoroughly to combine. Set aside until required.

Cut each cooled potato into six to eight wedges. Cut away most of the potato flesh, leaving about ½ inch of potato with the skin attached. Discard the potato flesh, or reserve for use in another recipe.

Heat some oil in a deep pan to a temperature of 350°F using a cooking thermometer. Deep-fry the potato skins in batches for 3-5 minutes, until they are crisp and golden. Remove from the oil with a slotted spoon, and drain on paper towels.

Serve the potato skins at once, accompanied by the dressing. SERVES 4-6

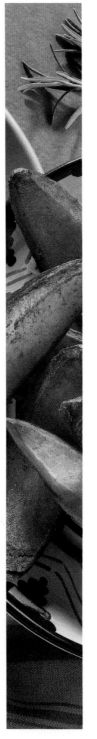

ROSEMARY & GARLIC POTATO WEDGES

4 large baking potatoes, weighing about
8 ounces each
1 cup extra virgin olive oil
2 teaspoons paprika
4 cloves garlic, crushed
3 tablespoons chopped fresh rosemary
Sea salt and freshly ground black pepper
Chili or Herb Mayonnaise (see page 12) or
Tomato Relish (see page 16), to serve

Preheat the oven to 400°F. Cut each potato into eight thin wedges, and place them on a large baking sheet. Mix together the oil, paprika, garlic and rosemary. Pour this mixture over the potatoes. Season the potatoes with salt and pepper, and toss well to make sure the potatoes are thoroughly coated in oil.

Bake the potatoes in the oven for 45 minutes, basting occasionally, until they are crisp and golden. Remove from the oven.

Serve at once with flavored mayonnaise or Tomato Relish. SERVES 4-6

TOP: Rosemary & Garlic Potato Wedges
BOTTOM: Potato Skins with
Sour Cream Dressing